HOW TO RESPECT EVEN IF YOU LEARNED DISRESPECT

Ten Practical Steps to Master Respect

JAMES E. PUCKETT

outskirts
press

ABOUT THE BOOK

The author recounts the time spent working with and around children and highlights in this self-help book one problem he experienced amongst many of them—disrespect. During these experiences, several life principles were noted missing in each of these children's lives. There are certain life principles that children must be taught. Learn what they are.

TABLE OF CONTENTS

Introduction   •   i

STEP 1
Change the way you think   •   1

STEP 2
Respect yourself first   •   5

STEP 3
Start early in learning to respect   •   9

STEP 4
Avoid negative influences   •   13

STEP 5
Train yourself through practice   •   17

STEP 6

Seize the first opportunity • 21

STEP 7

Learn how to deal
with life's interruptions • 25

STEP 8

Don't take offense to "No" answers • 29

STEP 9

Be responsible for your actions • 33

STEP 10

Always have an attitude of gratitude • 37

Conclusion • 41

About the Author • 47

INTRODUCTION

Let me start by saying that I have had the honor to work with and around some awesome teenagers during the past eighteen years. I know their parents are really proud of each of them. But at the same time, I have worked with and around some not so well-behaved adolescents. Many adolescents of this generation are rebellious, defiant, pernicious, and disrespectful. But because I am a somewhat of an optimistic person, I believe there is still hope for them.

We live in a time when wrong is seen as right, right is seen as wrong, good is seen as bad, and bad is seen as good. As I watch people come and go in their daily living, it amazes me how evil and corrupt this society is. As I work with and around teens, I am greatly concerned about where this great nation, the United States, is headed. As I travel about, watch television, listen to the radio, read the newspapers, and utilize other observational standpoints, I am disturbed by the actions and behaviors many of our teenagers are involved in. In my opinion, we are bringing up a generation of children that seeks to dominate their homes, their communities, and their schools. Until we as parents wake up and acknowledge that our children are being taught to live a self-destructive life, we will have the privilege of sharing in our children's self-destructive lifestyle. I am stirred in my spirit. This is not just a problem where I live, but it's a problem nationwide.

The family unit that I grew up knowing has diminished, and meanwhile homes, communities, and schools are elevated with evil. In our present society we have a role reversal going on. In today's society, many teens control what goes on in the home. Many of them tell their parents what they are going to do (or not do). I grew up thinking this was the role and responsibility of the parents. The way the families functioned back then—was it all wrong? Is it right the way many families operate today? I am glad I had someone to look after me and to tell me what was safe and unsafe, and to help me maneuver through this thing called "life". If I had been allowed to do my own thing and make my own decisions as a child, I would have gotten myself into jams that even my parents couldn't have gotten me out of. If parents are not raising their children today, then who—or what—is raising them? Children must be taught that there is a protocol for everything they choose to be involved in. Their conduct in life will be measured by the training they receive in their homes at the hands of their parents. The home is the primary place for teaching children how to behave in life. Schools are not responsible for teaching children how to behave, dress, or conduct themselves in public. Discipline starts at home. If children were all disciplined at home, then the schools wouldn't have to deal with so many behavior problems.

I will be the first to admit that I love today's technology. I own an iPod, which I use when I exercise. I have a cell phone equipped with camera and texting ability and probably have some features I am not aware of. I own one of the most up-to-date desktop computers and a laptop, which I can mobilize throughout the house and connect to the Internet from any room. There are so many good inventions that were meant to help man on earth, but which have also turned out to be some of the biggest downfall of man. Take the Internet, for example: one can find just about anything that he or she is looking for on the worldwide web. It is a great tool for researching and gathering information on just about any subject. One can post pictures and upload information to share with family and friends that live all across the world. One can search for employment and even post one's resume. Looking up addresses and phone numbers has never been easier. Law enforcement personnel use the Internet to track, catch, and convict criminals.

The cell phone and computer were designed to improve our way of life, but they have become some of the daily tools man has come to find addictive. The Internet has proven to be one of the worst tools at corrupting our teens.

The cell phone is another tool invented to help make our lives better. It was meant for healthy and moral communications purposes. But some people have taken the modern-day cell phone and turned it into a destructive tool. The use of cell phones in school has become one of the negative influences on the learning ability of students. Many students concentrate more on text and picture messaging than they do on schoolwork. The use of cell phones in schools has become a major distraction in classrooms. I believe that if students are allowed to have cell phones in school it should be for emergency purposes only. The cell phone should be off and out of sight and only taken out in case of an emergency. Some teens have discovered that they can send and receive both voice and text messages specifically designed to hurt their victims. In addition, we cannot forget about television, movies, videogames, and all the other different media outlets. Should we ignore these things and say, "These are just means of entertainment," or will we acknowledge that these negatively influence our kids?

The computer and cell phone are not bad tools of themselves. The problem lies in their use as a means to hurt, shame, and threaten others. These devices have a greater influence on children than their parents. Teachers, administrators, and security personnel all agree that these devices have a huge effect on the learning ability of students. Again, I ask who or what is teaching our children?

As I look at most adolescents today I wonder who or what are they modeling themselves after? A positive role model in the life of a child is very important. As I observe children, most of them view some celebrity figure as their role model. The problem with this is that some celebrities are not worthy to be called positive role models. Yet they are all a role model in some form or fashion. They all are teaching our children something, whether it's good or bad, right or wrong. Our children need to be associated with people who will present themselves in a positive manner toward them.

I didn't always know what I am about to say, but I think the parents should be their children's first choice for their role model – the first that he or she will set eyes on. One would hope that the parents would be that positive role model. As I've gotten older and wiser, I have realized the influence that my parents had on me as a child. Of course, in my younger years I didn't view this as being important, but now that I am married and have a family of my own, I understand the importance of having that positive example for children. When I think about the functions of a role model, I think about someone who has integrity, honesty, loyalty, and who is loving and hardworking, and a provider. As I look back on my childhood, I can see all these and more in my parents. My parents were my positive role models and it was a choice that both Mom and Dad made, even though I didn't know it at the time. So I say, "Thank you, Dad and Mom!" I think I turned out pretty good.

When it comes to teaching children what's right and what's wrong, it must be done with respect toward the child, and it must be done with consistency. Children must know and understand why something is considered right or wrong, and I believe it is the parent's responsibility to teach his or her child the "whys" of right and wrong, try to answer their questions and to help them understand. I believe the way every parent will go about this process must be given careful thought beforehand. I have learned, both from working with and around children for the past eighteen years and from my studies in earning my Master's degree in counseling, that adolescents are less likely to reject information when it is shared as a part of small talk. This creates continuity in the relationship. Waiting until they make the wrong choice is not the time, in my opinion, to talk to a child about right and wrong. I believe that when parents choose to make small talk with their children, a bond develops between them, and children will openly talk and ask questions. That bond should be understood as a parent-child and a child-parent relationship. When a child makes the choice to break the law and ends up behind bars, it's a little too late to lecture him or her on drinking and driving or on the company they keep. Answering the "whys" for your children, I believe, will help them make wise choices when they are faced with the uncertainties of life.

When parents fail to teach their children right from wrong, the children will come to their own conclusions as to what is right or wrong based on their surroundings and on influences from others. Doing what's wrong doesn't just stem from wrong teaching; it can also come from a lack of teaching. Teaching young people to make the right choices is imperative to help them avoid adopting false or wrong conclusions about life's challenges. When false or wrong conclusions are developed from a child's experiences, they will always have trouble distinguishing right from wrong. This is why I believe children must be taught as early as possible about right and wrong.

One may ask the question: "How early is as early as possible?" I remember as a little boy, still in diapers, I would get my little hands, legs, and bottom slapped whenever I exercised any type of negative behavior. Did I understand why I was getting such attention at first? No! But if I continued my negative behavior, the slapping became more intense and forceful and consequently, over time, I learned that such negative behaviors would not be accepted, at least, not in the presence of my father and mother.

Children learn early in life how to manipulate their parents and others so they can get their way. Many small children are pros at redirecting their parents' attempts to deny them what they desire. Children who receive overwhelming attention through poor behavior, without any negative consequences, quickly learn how far they can go and what it takes to get their way. And believe me, they will push, push, and keep on pushing until someone gives in. It's normally the parent.

I have witnessed young children in public places, some still in their training pants and barely able to walk, use the word "No" to reject something their parents just told them. The child knows to make such a fuss to the point that the parents give in, which reinforces the child's methods of using poor behavior to get their way. I watch and listen, thinking, *If that child is not corrected now, he will grow up displaying the same negative behavior; perhaps with an even more forceful approach to getting his way.*

So, when is "as early as possible" early enough? This will obviously depend on the child and the environment. I believe correction and parental intervention should begin as soon there are signs of negative behaviors. If small children are old enough to form the word "No" in their mind and speak it aloud, I believe they are also capable of understanding what they are saying, why they are saying it, and what they expect to gain from it.

Too often, we as parents look at this type of negative behavior and do not give it serious thought because the child is so small. We may even find it funny at times. However, children recognize this response and, over time, they will also find humor in their own negative behavior. The more laughs and attention they get for the negative behavior, the more frequent and intensive the behavior becomes.

I am concerned that today's average family unit has allowed the pendulum of its child behavior to go too far to the left or right. There must be a balance taught in a child's life. I believe that too much exposure to one thing and not enough to others will teach a child what is viewed as acceptable and unacceptable. If a child is allowed to grow up exposed to too much of the way the world lives, their life will consist of the same. Allowing children to be exposed to certain types of things too early will infect their minds, which could lead to self-destruction later. This is why I believe it is vitally important that parents start to teach their children as early as possible. The more opportunities a child has to explore what society has to offer, without regulations, the harder it becomes to reach them. I am not suggesting that parents should try and shield their children from normal experiences, but I do believe that parents ought to monitor what their children are exposed to and should teach that balance is necessary for a healthy lifestyle.

A child is born into this world knowing nothing. If a parent fails to teach his or her child about right and wrong while they are young, this leaves them without some of the necessary principles of life, which could cause them to self-destruct later. Consequently, the child will go through life, however long that is, self-destructing.

STEP

1

CHANGE THE WAY YOU THINK

For as he thinketh in his heart, so is he:
Eat and drink, saith he to thee; but his
heart is not with thee
(Proverbs 23:7).

- Your life will go in the direction of your
  thoughts.

The ways we think about life in general have a great deal to do with how we feel about ourselves and others. This is important because if we have wrong thinking, we don't care about ourselves or anyone else. Believe it or not, how a person thinks becomes their reality. "As a man thinketh in his heart, so is he."

When we get our mind right and begin to think positively, that is when we start to unlock the treasures inside us. Our mind will play tricks on us. When we start to think right, the treasures deep inside us will start to surface.

To change the way you think, you must first change what you are saying about yourself. What are you saying about yourself? Are you repeating the negative things that have been told to you all your life? Are you saying about you what others are saying about you? Some of those negative things being said about you might be true, but you can change them by what you say about you. You properly won't be able to change what happened in the past, but you can change how you proceed into the future. What you think about you will determine whether you will respect or disrespect yourself or those around you.

When you start to believe in yourself, you start to respect life and the challenges that come with it. Notice I didn't say "enjoy life." No one enjoys a challenge but we all should embrace challenges. Challenges, if we approach them with the right perspective, should change how we think. You will be amazed how your life will look so much brighter and more promising when you change how you think. You start to believe in you, and most important, you start to respect yourself, others, and life in general—which leads us to step # 2.

STEP
2

RESPECT YOURSELF FIRST

Master, which is the great command-
ment in the law? Jesus said unto him,
Thou shalt love the Lord thy God with all
thy heart, and with all thy soul, and with
all thy mind. This is the first and great
commandment
(Matthew 22:36-38).

- Practice Self-Love and Self-Respect.

Love and respect go together like hand and glove. Before you can be taught to respect others, you must first learn to respect yourself. This is so important. But one must learn to love himself before he can respect himself. This is not a prideful love or an arrogant love. It's a Godly type of love. I believe this is why people, especially children, react in such a negative way when they are confronted with any type of authority. An act of showing love will translate into an act of showing respect. When love for oneself is not present, respect for oneself or others is not present. Love and respect for oneself should start in the home. It is the responsibility of parents to teach their children to respect themselves.

First, you must recognize and accept you are different and unique. Many times children will look at others in their age group and desire to have the same or similar talents or gifts as their friends or acquaintances. You must realize and accept that you are of a different character, have different talents or gifts, and most of all, your creator, God, said you are uniquely made.

Loving and respecting yourself first is a prerequisite for respecting authority and the property of others. All the negative things you are subject to, either by words or actions, you will remember for the rest of your life. In many cases, this is where the positive mental growth of a child stops. This is why many children have a problem respecting authority—they were never taught to love. Before you can respect authority at any level, you must first love and respect yourself.

Loving and respecting yourself leads to loving and respecting others and their property. So it is simple: loving and respecting oneself at all times will lead to loving and respecting others and what belongs to them.

STEP

3

START EARLY IN LEARNING TO RESPECT

I love them that love me; and those that seek me early shall find me
(Proverbs 8:17).

- What you learn or are taught early in life will be some of the same behaviors you practice the rest of your life.

I believe it's important to seek God and His biblical plan for His children early in life. Like most things in life, the longer we procrastinate, the harder it becomes to change or correct something. The longer we put off doing what we know is right and continue to do it the way we have always done it, the more difficult it is to change. Some people find it almost impossible to change. Seeking God early, in my opinion, will provide for a better way of life, not only in your early years but also in your later years, and will also help establish a firm foundation for the journey of your life.

The behavior patterns we learn or are taught when we are young will be practiced or lived out in our later years. This is one reason why children grow up to be like their parents. It's not all genetic. A lot of what we do and how we act in our later years is taught or picked up from our parents or some other family member or friend.

Intervention is vital when the negative behavior of disrespect is shown. Early intervention is important because it has a greater chance of reversing negative behaviors that lead to disrespect. Failure to do this will affect decision-making skills, especially in choosing right over wrong, and it also affects how you relate to others—respecting them or disrespecting them.

You will need the support of others. Most children don't realize that they need someone to intervene in their life and many will reject it when it comes, but intervention will redirect a child's behavior. Children need this support from parents and other authority figures. If they are left to grow up without intervention, they will learn from lack of intervention and negative teaching to disrespect everyone and everything around them.

STEP

4

AVOID NEGATIVE INFLUENCES

Blessed is the man that walketh not in the counsel of the ungodly, nor standeth in the way of sinners, nor sitteth in the seat of the scornful.

But his delight is in the law of the Lord; and in his law doth he meditate day and night.

And he shall be like a tree planted by the rivers of water, that bringeth forth his fruit in his season; his leaf also shall not wither; and whatsoever he doeth shall prosper.

The ungodly are not so: but are like the chaff which the wind driveth away.

Therefore the ungodly shall not stand in the judgment, nor sinners in the congregation of the righteous.

For the Lord knoweth the way of the righteous: but the way of the ungodly shall perish
(Psalms 1:1-6).

My son, if sinners entice thee, consent thou not
(Proverbs 1:10).

- Negative influences will cause friction between respect and disrespect.

"Misery loves company." We cannot keep company with people who think differently from us. If your goal is to master how to respect at every opportunity, then it is imperative that you not associate with people who don't respect or practice respect. If you have associates and friends whose lives revolve around negative behavior and your goal is to practice respect, there will always be tension between you and them.

Negative influences are destructive. Negative influences will create wrong ideas and thoughts in the mind. Negative influences will cause you to go places and do things you thought you would never go or do. People or things that you may have been taught to respect, you will now find yourself disrespecting. If you allow yourself to be controlled by negative influences it will ruin your life and those of the people around you. The result is you have no respect for yourself, others, or life. You self-destruct right before your own eyes and you don't even realize what is happening to you until it is too late.

Negative influences have driving forces behind them. I use the word "driving" because that's what negative influences are compared to. They take you places you would not have gone on your own—places you probably don't want to go or never intended to go. Negative influences have a controlling force attached to them that causes a person to act in a way that they don't even understand. This force is uncontrollable by the one being controlled. It's like getting in your car and driving to get from point A to B. Negative influences will drive you to think one way when you know you should be thinking another way. Negative influences will drive one to negative behaviors, which result in the behavior of disrespect. Why not get behind the wheel of your own life and drive your own destiny? For a better quality of life, deny yourself all negative influences and start practicing respect today.

STEP

5

TRAIN YOURSELF THROUGH PRACTICE

Take heed unto thyself, and unto the doctrine; continue in them: for in doing this thou shalt both save thyself, and them that hear thee
(1 Timothy 4:16).

- Mastering respect comes through practice.

I like this passage of Scripture from First Timothy. It challenges us to check ourselves and to be careful about what we are taught and whom we are taught by. This is why I started out by stating that respect is taught and disrespect is learned. First we must make sure we are being taught by the right people, and second, we must make sure they are teaching us the right thing.

The word "continue" in the above Scripture literally means ongoing, continuous, sustained, persistent, steady, and relentless—well, you get the picture. You could say "practice" and it would mean the same thing.

Practice! Practice! Practice! Practice will take discipline on your part. Through individual practice, with respect, you will learn self-discipline.

The practice never ends. While you are learning something new or are being taught something new, you must continue to practice to get better at it. Mastering respect must be practiced over and over again. There is never an end to it. What you appreciate, you will continue to respect. The practice in respect never ends because your goal is to master how to respect. So it's a lifelong task. It becomes a lifestyle.

The practice is unconditional. It does not matter what the conditions or situations are, practicing respect is the objective. It does not matter what everyone else around you is doing or not doing. It does not matter if you feel like doing it or not. It does not matter what someone may have done to you. Your goal is to master how to respect, therefore you cannot place conditions on when to respect and when not to respect. In my opinion, respect always sends a positive message, even if we feel or think no respect is warranted.

It is important for us to practice respect because doing so will save us from much heartache in life and when others hear and see us practicing respect, it teaches them that respecting is the right way to live their life, which will save them from self-destructing.

SEIZE THE FIRST OPPORTUNITY

*As we have therefore opportunity, let us
do good unto all men, especially unto
them who are of the household of faith*
(Galatians 6:10).

- Look for every opportunity to show
  respect.

Look for opportunities to show respect. A good place to start is with yourself, then in your home. Start with your parents. Take every opportunity to show respect for them and what they have done for you and are doing for you. Another good place is your school. I am sure your principals and teachers will love it. Even where you worship, where you shop and where you work are great places to show respect as the opportunity presents itself. Everywhere you go and in everything you do there will be opportunities to show respect. Even if you think someone or something does not deserve your respect, do it anyway. Your goal is to master doing it.

Opportunities will never cease, no matter how many times or how long you practice this—the opportunities will always be there. They will never cease and neither should you. The more opportunities you look for to show respect, the more you will find them. But there will be times when opportunities present themselves and you did not look for them, nor did you expect them. These are critical times when practicing respect is essential.

Opportunities will come, large and small. Don't just look for the special opportunities or the ones where you are expected to show respect, but seize every opportunity even if you are not sure, no matter how insufficient the opportunities may seem.

STEP

7

LEARN HOW TO DEAL WITH LIFE'S INTERRUPTIONS

And if it seem evil unto you to serve the Lord, choose you this day whom ye will serve; whether the gods which your fathers served that were on the other side of the flood, or the gods of the Amorites, in whose land ye dwell: but as for me and my house, we will serve the Lord (Joshua 24:15).

- Challenges will come and could interrupt your plans or goals.

Staying the course after you have made the decision to master respect will ultimately come down to a personal commitment. Challenges will come but you should learn from them. I am sure Joshua had many reasons to confess a different statement, but he chose the one that he knew would bring him and his family the best outcome. He made the decision and told the people it was in their best interest to not do as their fathers had done. As a result of his decision, the people agreed with him. You could say that Joshua was influential in their decision.

Challenges sometimes are "setbacks," but do not allow them to turn into "holdbacks." Interruptions in our already-planned-out day can sometimes make us want to put our plans and goals on hold or give up on them altogether.

If it is determined that the interruption came as a result of a problem, then the goal is to solve the problem as soon as possible. Some problems will be more easily solved than others. But do not allow the challenges of the problem to interrupt you from your ultimate outcome. Challenges brought on by interruptions should challenge you to look for more reasons to show respect.

You have to plan and make it your goal to show respect and let nothing get in the way of that plan. Your plan is to show respect no matter what is going on in your life or around you. Your goal is to take every opportunity to respect, every minute of the day and whenever the opportunity is there.

Learn to respect the interruptions. Interruptions are just what they say they are: "interruptions." The interruptions come to stop you, slow you up, or completely stall you in advancing your plan and goal. Make the choice to choose to respect no matter if others around you refuse to. You are working toward an end result—Mastering Respect.

STEP

8

DON'T TAKE OFFENSE TO "NO" ANSWERS

For where envying and strife is, there is confusion and every evil work
(James 3:16).

- You should always respect a "No" answer.

Most people tend to get a little disappointed when they are told "No" to a question or situation where they were expecting or hoping for a "Yes." I believe this is a common reaction for most people. Some might even become angry and take on an offensive spirit behind it. This is a sure-fire way of inviting strife into the situation. I don't know too many people who can show respect when they are in strife with one another. When you are told "No" try to see things from the other person's perspective.

Take your parents, for instance. Think of a time when they issued you a "No" to something you had your heart set on. How did it make you feel? Did it make you want to rebel against them? Did it make you want to talk back to them? Did you get a little bit of an attitude? Did you become offensive toward them?

This is especially important for teens. When your parents or people in a position of authority tell you "No" about something, it usually means they know what's in your best interest or at the least have more knowledge about the issue.

Respect the "No" answers and you will be better off in the long run.

Being told "No" doesn't always mean never. Realizing this at the outset will give you a better understanding at that moment and you will appreciate and respect the "No" and the person behind the "No" at that time and later on in life

Receive every "No" as a learning experience. Just like challenges, receiving a "No" answer is an opportunity to show respect even if you don't fully understand the reason for the "No." You are being told "No" for a reason. Learn why, then accept it and respect it, because it won't be your last one. You getting upset probably will not change anything and it will hold you back from your ultimate plan and goal. Being told "No" could be a way of saying this is not for you or at least not at this time. Respect it and move on.

Being told "No" might have you a little confused, but don't allow it to get you into evil works. Evil works and respect are like oil and water; the two don't mix.

STEP

9

BE RESPONSIBLE FOR YOUR ACTIONS

Talk no more so exceeding proudly; let not arrogancy come out of your mouth: for the Lord is a God of knowledge, and by him actions are weighed
(1 Samuel 2:3).

- Your actions are yours.

When we fail to take responsibility for our actions, we by default place the responsibility on something or someone else. Our actions matter to God and they should matter to us. We must examine them and place blame where blame is due.

In the passage of Scripture above the word "weigh" means "examine." In one translation it reads "appraised." Our actions are examined or appraised by God. God places a value on the things that we say and do, whether they are good or bad, and expects us to do the same.

Be responsible for the good and bad *you* cause in your life. Notice I said "You." If you know you caused the problem, own up to it. You will not be examined or appraised for someone else's actions. The quicker you do, the quicker you can get on with life. Not being responsible for your actions is really disrespecting yourself and the person or thing you are holding responsible. An irresponsible person is an unthankful person. An unthankful person is a disrespectful person.

While you are on your new journey of mastering respect, some good things will happen to you which will be easy to respect, and some not-so-good things will happen to you that will be not so easy to respect. Remember, there are no conditions for showing respect. Not placing conditions on respecting must be a prerequisite to mastering respect.

Taking personal responsibility will not always seem like the respectful thing to do but it's the right thing to do. Claim it as soon as you realize you have caused it. Don't wait for someone else to claim responsibility for it. Don't wait for someone to point it out to you. As soon as you realize you have made a mistake, own it. Doing this will prove you are responsible and respect how others might be affected by your actions. If you get this one right, respect for others and other things will come much easier. This is not a popular thing with most people. But you are not like most people. You are on a mission with a goal and enjoying a new way of living.

STEP

10

ALWAYS HAVE AN ATTITUDE OF GRATITUDE

Giving thanks always for all things unto
God and the Father in the name of our
Lord Jesus Christ
(Ephesians 5:20).

- Your attitude has influence.

Showing thanksgiving is a way of respecting what God has done in your life. If we all were to take a moment and consider the alternatives, it should cause us to have an attitude of gratitude. I don't care what is going on in your life; God is bigger than your problem and understands your situation better than you do. People who are disrespectful will find it very hard to show gratitude for the people and things in their life. Even very successful people who have accomplished a lot in their life sometimes have difficulty being thankful for how far they have come. Some of these same people are so disrespectful that they would not give you the time of day. They have no respect for the people who are not on their level.

Your attitude will determine how you look, think, and feel. A bad attitude will not show any signs of gratitude. When there is no gratitude, there is no respect. When you have a heart of gratitude you will feel as though you are obligated to show respect. Your attitude will reflect that and others will show you respect. An attitude of gratitude will have an influence on others and will ultimately cause them to show respect to you and others. Your attitude is important. You have to start to look at life through a new set of eyes.

CONCLUSION

Respect is taught. Disrespect is learned. When respect is not taught, disrespect becomes the learned behavior. If a person is not taught how to respect, they will automatically learn disrespect through negative behaviors. Disrespect automatically comes as a result of failure to show respect.

Some parents choose to remain silent and not invade their children's space. They leave their child to learn from other sources. Being silent will cause parents and their children a whole lot of trouble in life. It's true they are learning, but are they learning what we, as parents, want them to learn? Your child's discovery could be fatal if they are left to learn on their own about the things of life in their adolescent and teen years. Because some children can be so vocal and strong-willed against their parents' policies and rules, many parents refuse to get involved in their child's life. How did we get here?

Often we, as parents, go through life with the perception that experience is the best teacher for our children. I will be the first to agree that experience can and will teach one a whole lot, but it is not the best teacher for your child. In my experience, parents are the best teachers. But could it be that this is where part of our problems with rebellious, defiant, and disrespectful children originate? How did we get here?

Could it be that the parents of these children who are rebellious, defiant, and disrespectful were never taught lessons on obedience and respect themselves? Parents who find themselves in this situation should seek help. No child should have to overcome life's obstacles by finding out the hard way. We, as parents, owe our children the opportunity to live a productive life. When a child is not taught to respect and obey authority, it usually leads to an unproductive and self-destructive lifestyle.

There was a time in our society when one could see and hear respect without even looking for it, but times have changed. In today's society, respect has to be demanded, and even when it is, most people don't know what it looks like or sounds like. Some people don't know if there is such thing as respect. This is why parents must start early teaching their children the importance of respect toward them as parents, for those in authority and for the property of others.

Many people don't respect the constitutional rights of others, yet they demand that their own rights not be violated. Many people don't respect the property of others and will, many times, go out of their way to possess what is not theirs. Children who challenge law enforcement personnel and others in positions of authority were never taught to show respect and obey authority at any level. Because they were never taught to respect, consequently, they have no respect for themselves or any type of authority. How did we get here?

If we, as parents, fail to teach our children the importance of respect while they are young, it could be our own children who later commit violence against us, in our own community, on our own streets and in our own homes. Many times, the children who pollute our streets with drugs and gangs were born and raised in the very houses they are menacing. How did we get here?

If someone wants what you have badly enough, they will stop at nothing to get it. We hear about this type of behavior going on every day around the world. Where is the respect for mankind? Self-worth for many people ceases to exist. Therefore, their self-worth for others cannot be shown. How did we get here? I guess the more important question would be how do we get back?

As we look throughout this nation, this country, in our cities, in our communities, and even in our homes, we witness a generation of lawless human beings. There is no regard for the rules of law that have been established. Laws are made to establish a rule of order. We have raised a generation of people who do not respect the laws that are supposed to govern our way of living. Someone once said, "If people are allowed to continue with their negative behaviors, they will always think that is the way they should behave and that it's the right way." How did we get there? Again, the question is, how do we get back to a people who respect the laws that are intended to ensure order in our society?

Coming from a military background, I believe that any organization or individual will fight the way it is trained. The family is an organization, and when the children leave home they are now in hand-to-hand combat in the world; they are going against forces that seem designed to destroy them. Lyndon Baines Johnson, the thirty-sixth president of the United States, once said, "The family is the cornerstone of our society. More than any other force, it shapes the attitude, the hope, the ambitions, and the values of our child."

It's time for parents and leaders to join in the battle and present our children with the knowledge they will need to help them live a better quality of life. It's time our children are taught the fundamentals of respect.

I believe it starts with us! This is the main reason I have written books that focus on the younger generation. If we are to change a generation of disrespectful people, we have to work at it.

ABOUT THE AUTHOR

JAMES PUCKETT is a retired Chief Warrant Officer Four (CW4) from the United States Army, with nearly twenty-five years of active duty service.

He has worked with and around adolescents and teens for the past eighteen years. Eight of those years he worked as a school security officer in a public high school. He currently holds a position as the Transportation Safety Officer for the school district.

He resides in Knoxville, Tennessee, with his wife Brenda. James holds a Master of Arts degree in pastoral counseling with concentrations in crisis intervention/child and family brief therapy from Liberty University Theological Seminary.

Lightning Source UK Ltd.
Milton Keynes UK
UKHW020408260620
365567UK00006B/924